This Book Belongs To:

____

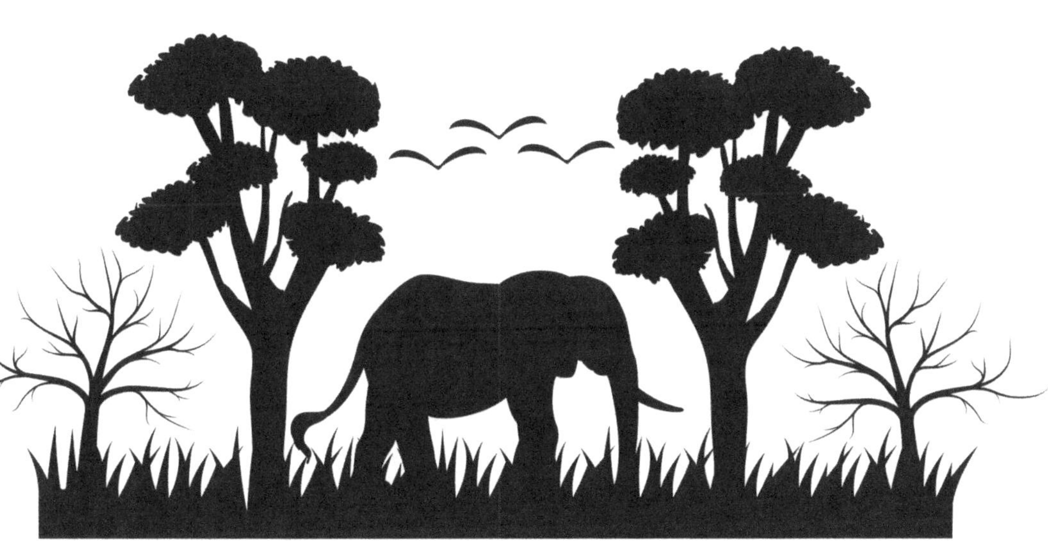

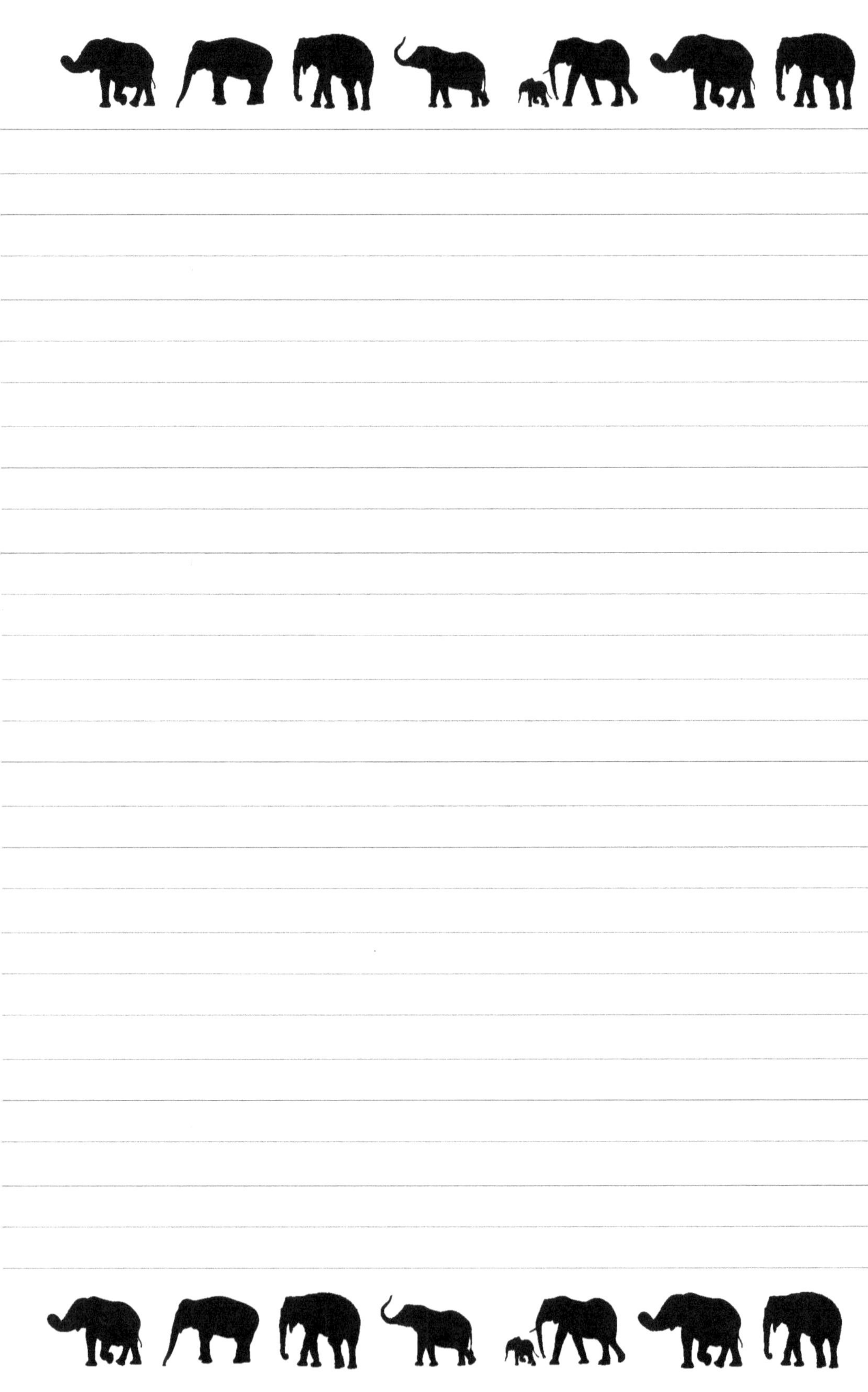

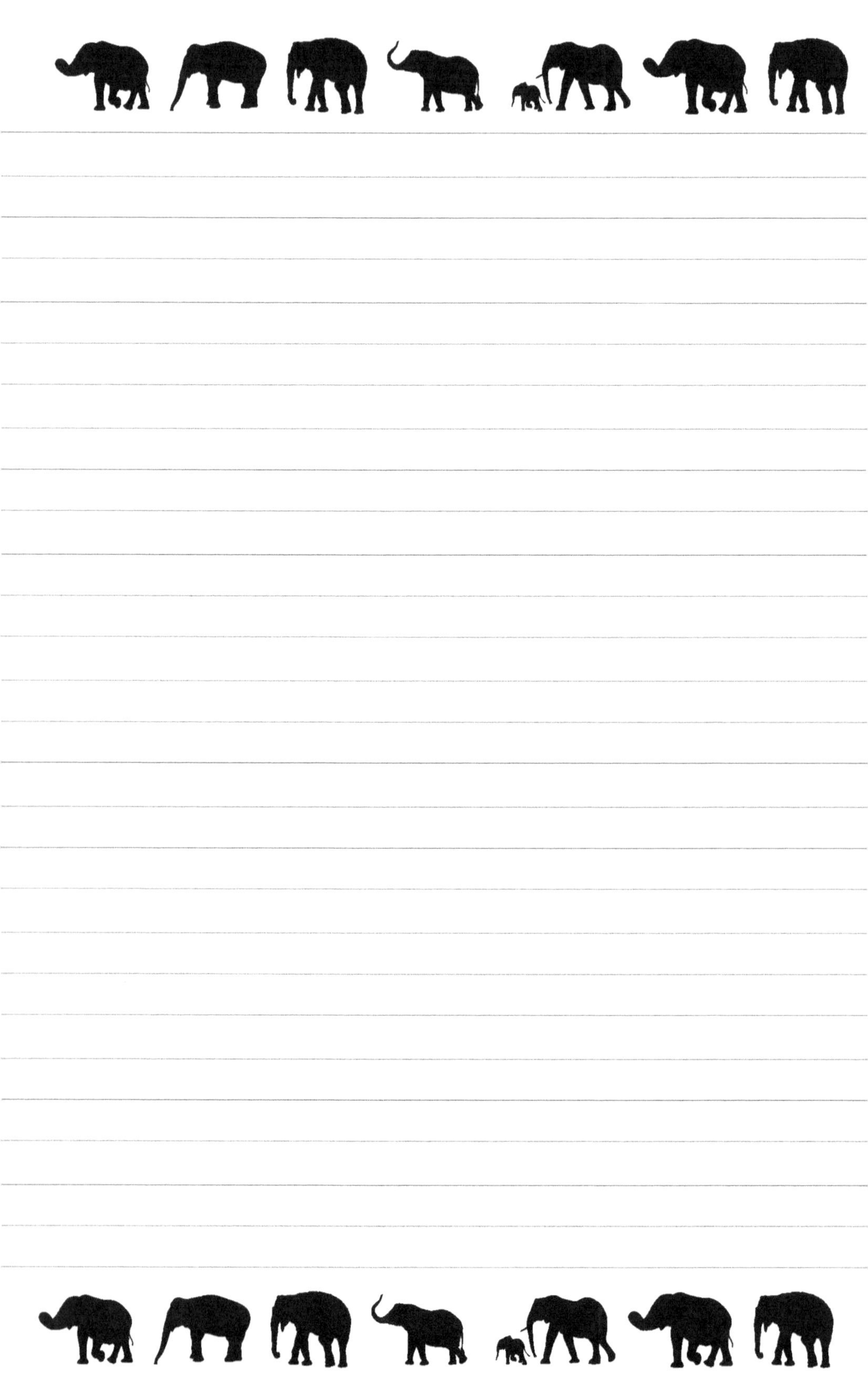

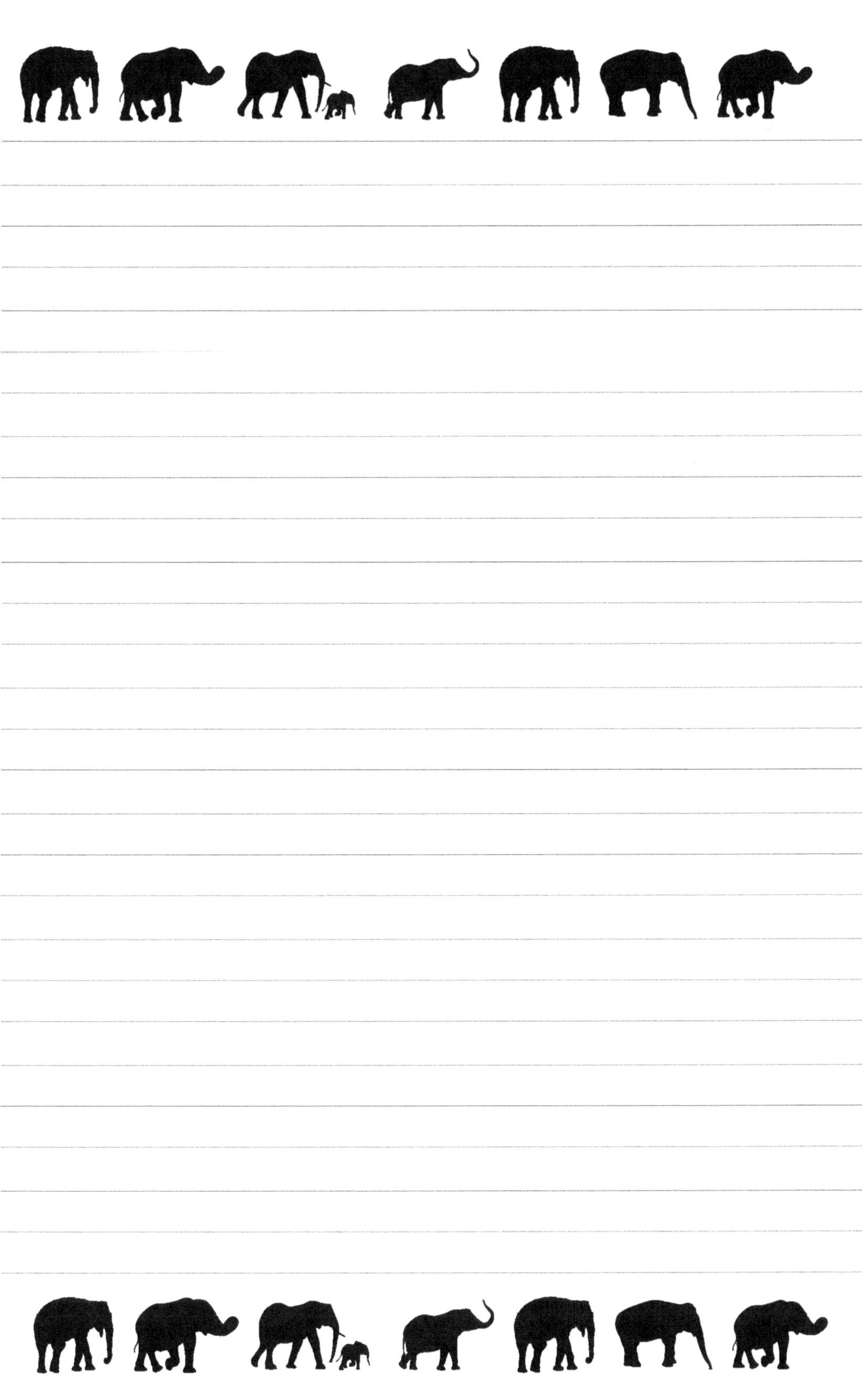

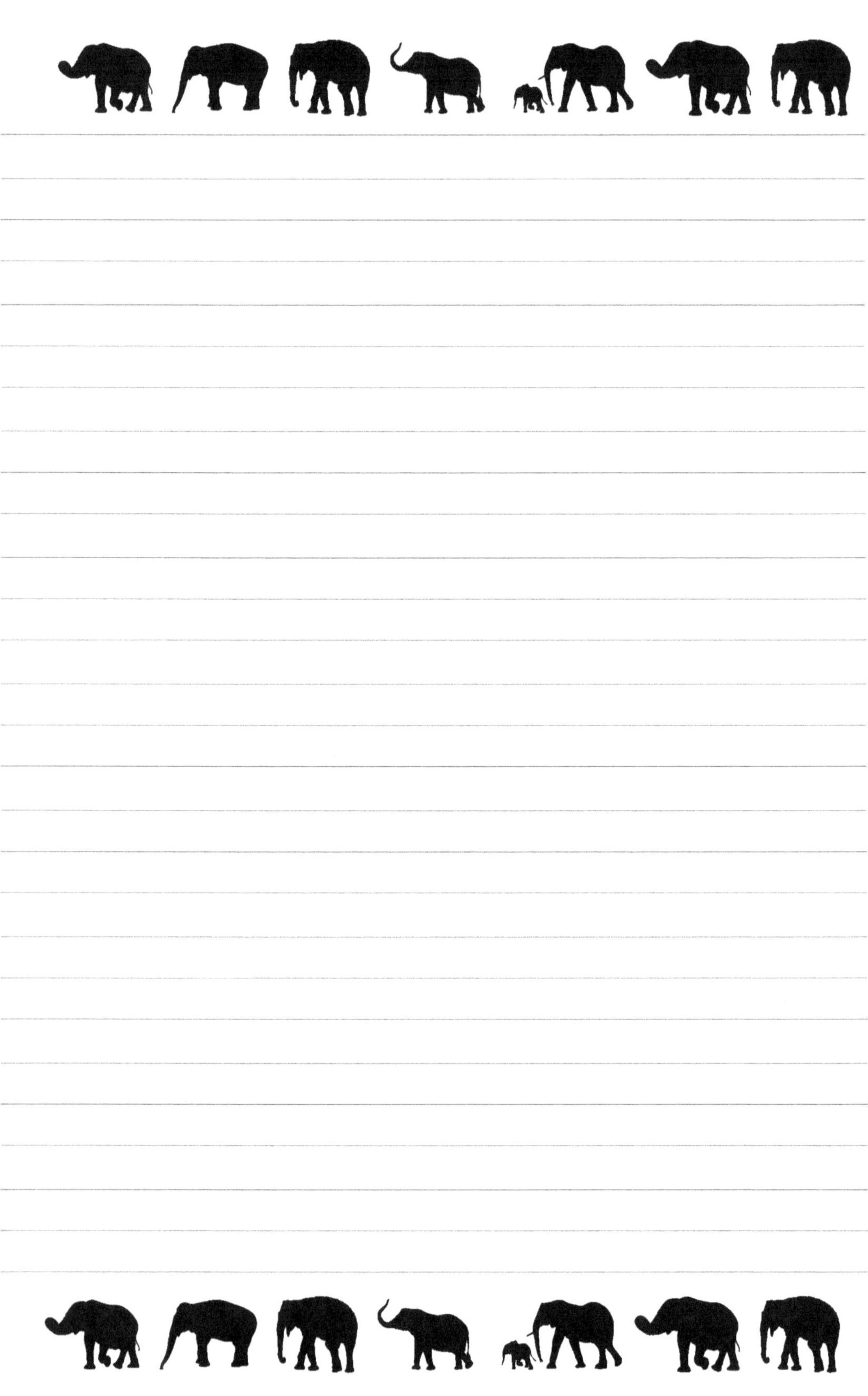

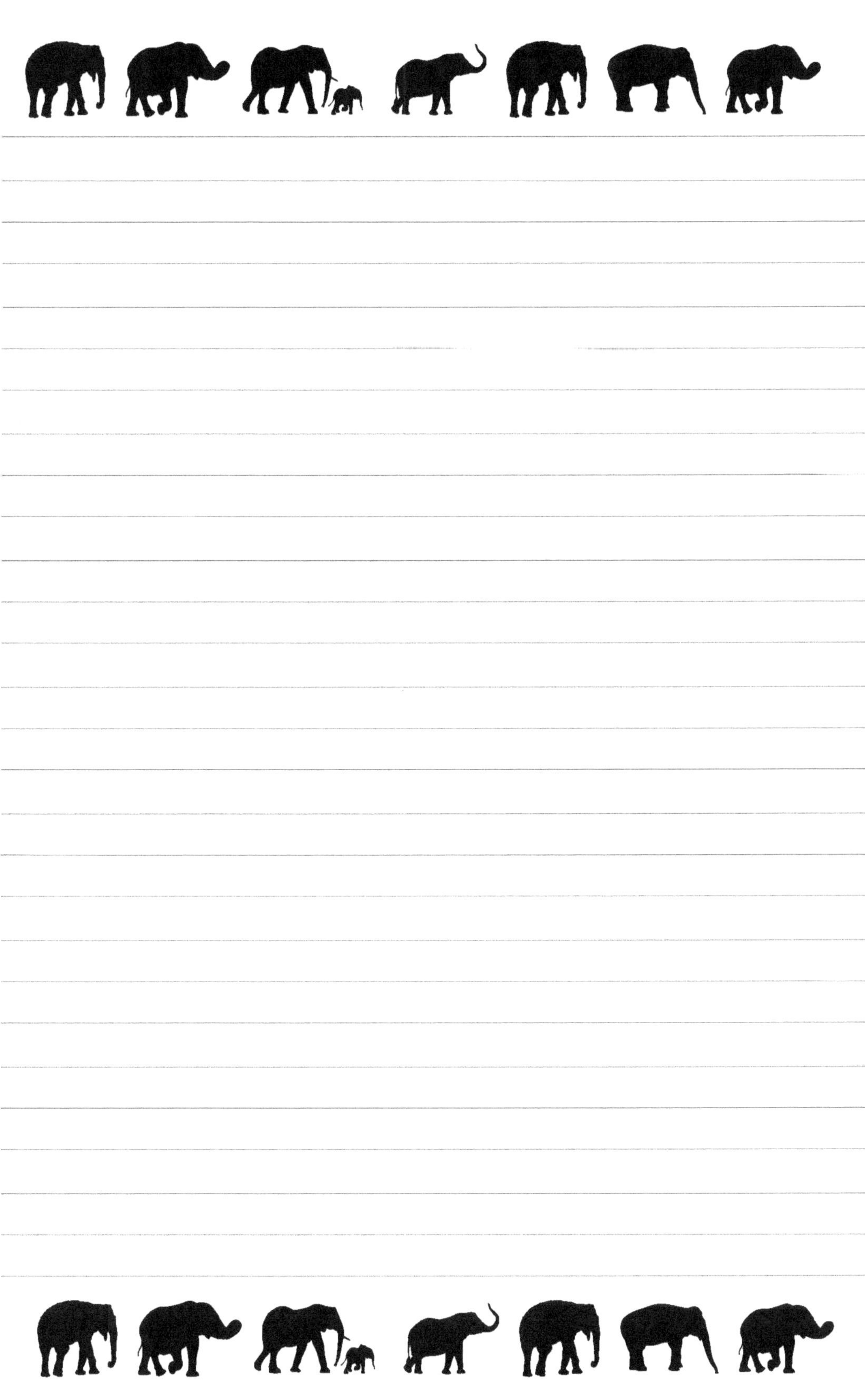

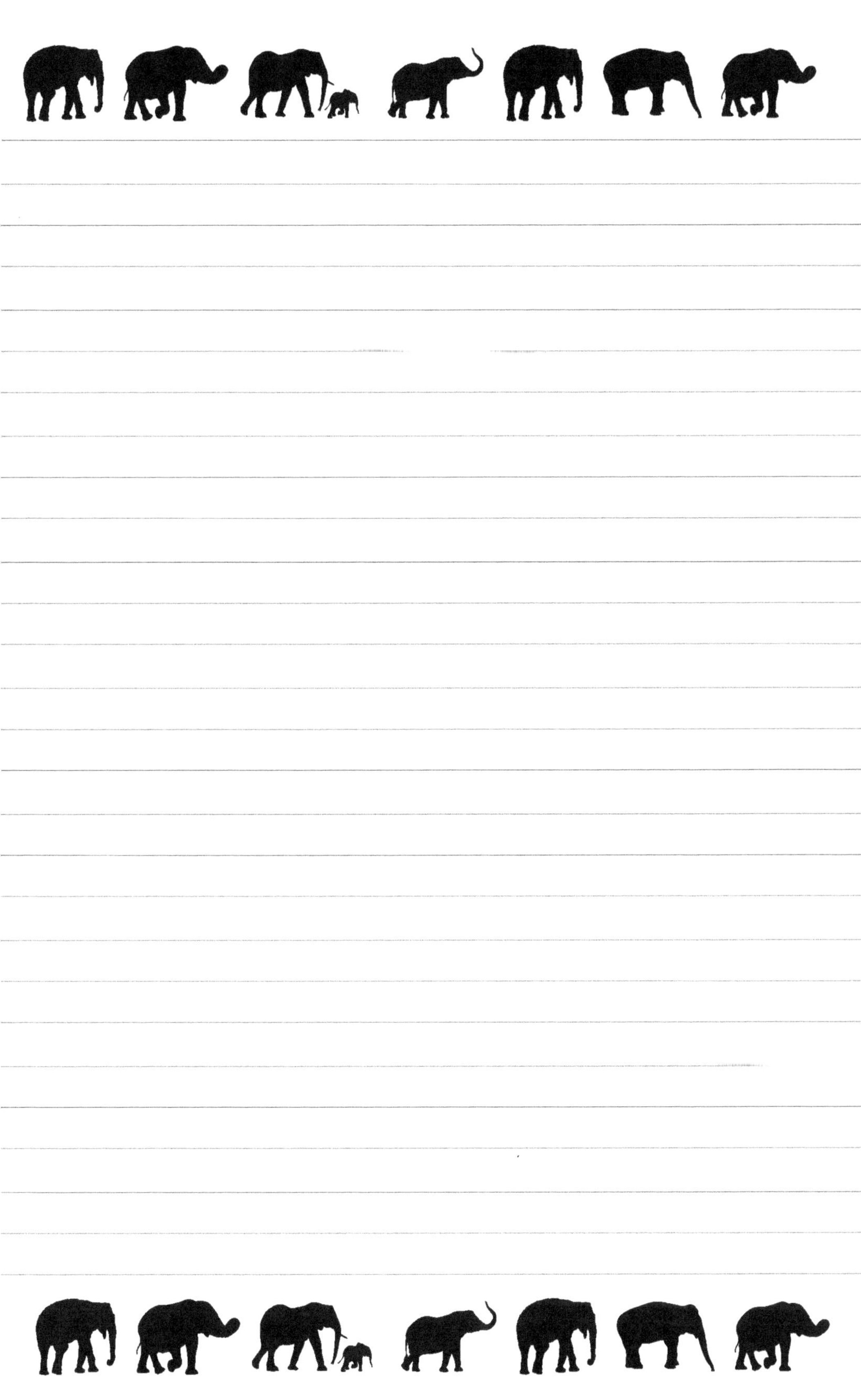

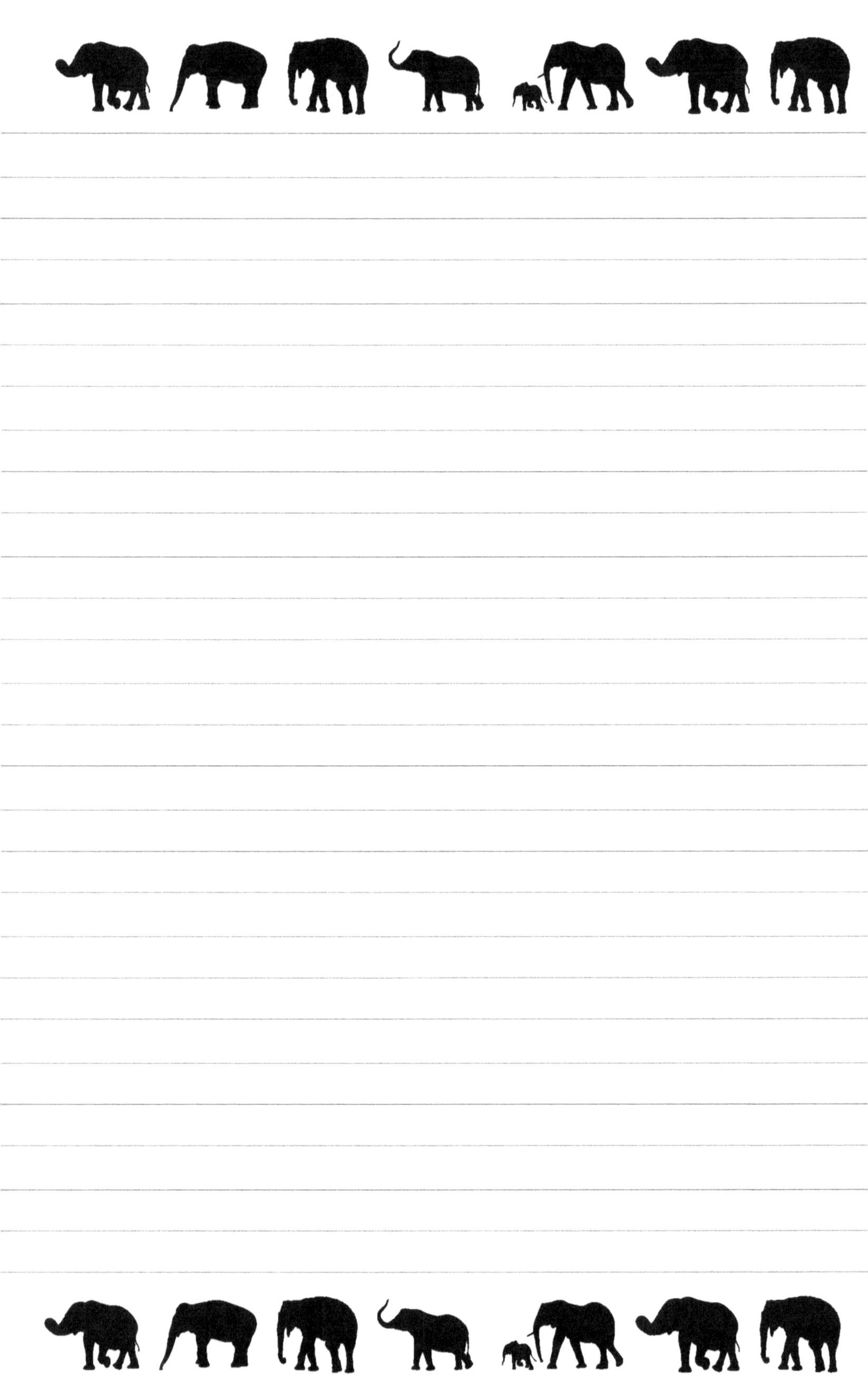

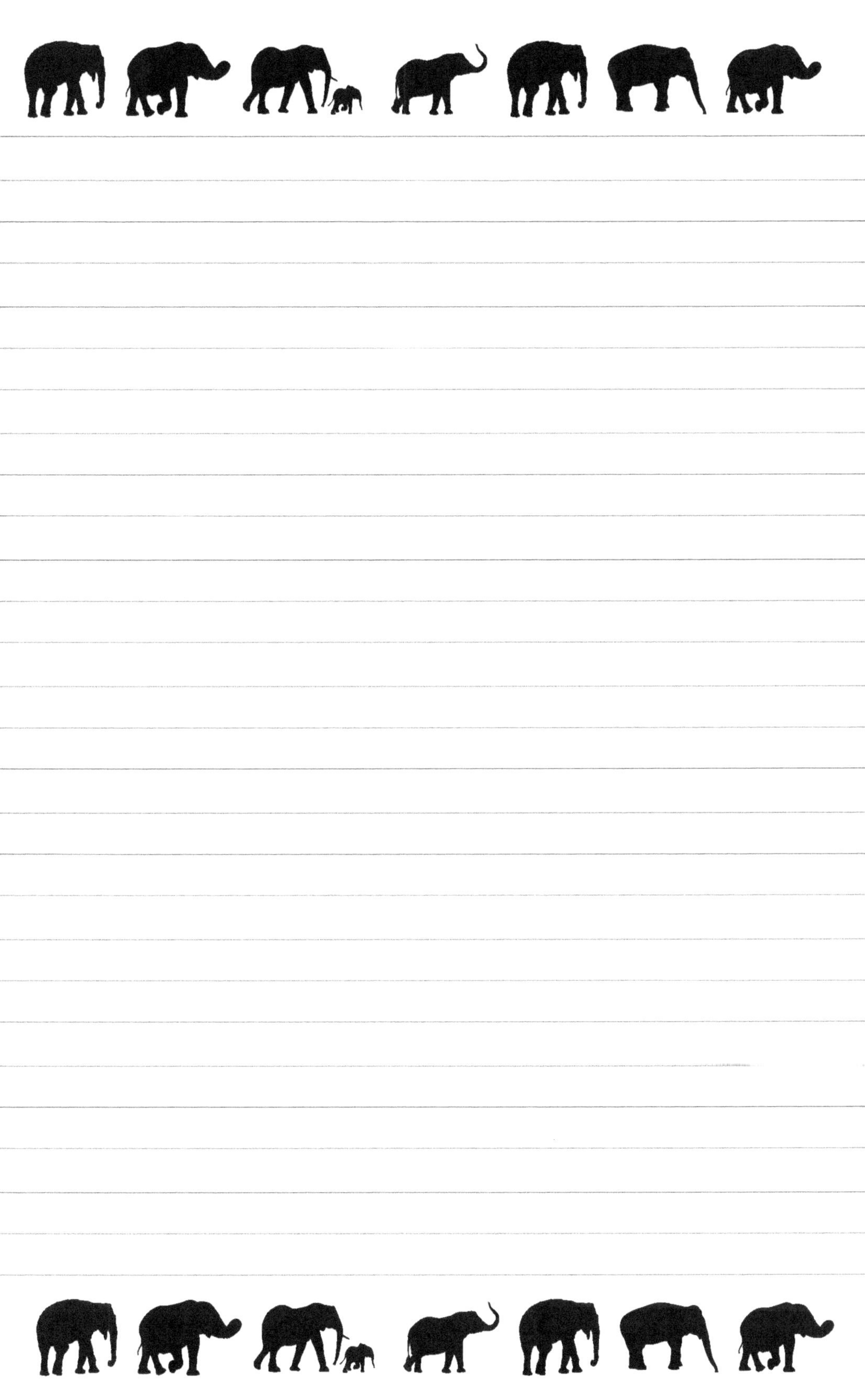